early MORNING VISITOR

A Daily Visitation with the Holy Spirit

early MORNING VISITOR

A Daily Visitation with the Holy Spirit

ROLINDA BUTLER

COOKE HOUSE PUBLISHING
WINSTON SALEM

EARLY MORNING VISITOR
Copyright © 2016 – Rolinda Butler

All rights reserved. This book is protected by the copyright laws of the United States of America. This book may not be copied or reprinted for commercial gain or profit. The use of quotations or occasional page copying for personal or group study is permitted and encouraged. Permission will be granted upon request.

Unless otherwise identified, Scripture quotations are from the King James Version. Copyright © 1982 by Thomas Nelson, Inc. Used by permission. All rights reserved.

Design by Cooke Consulting & Creations LLC
Cover Design: Tia W. Cooke

Soft cover ISBN: 978-0-9979923-0-4
eBook ISBN: 978-0-9979923-1-1

Library of Congress Cataloging-in-Publication Data
Names: Butler, Rolinda
Title: Early morning visitor: a daily visitation with the Holy Spirit / Rolinda Butler; LCCN: 2016952664
LC record available at https://lccn.loc.gov/2016952664

Cooke House Publishing
(a division of Cooke Consulting & Creations, LLC)
Winston-Salem, NC
publishing@cookecc.org

This book and all Cooke House Publishing books are available at Christian bookstores and distributors worldwide.

Printed in the United States of America.- First Edition

Dedication

For me it started here. My grandmother, Nicie Goode, was a very quiet and soft spoken woman who seemed to have mastered humility with excellence. Even through her test I believed she trusted God. I never heard her really get loud or raise her voice even when angry. She loved and I am hoping she felt loved. What can I say about her? Well, I can say she was there for me.

I truly want to dedicate this book to the Glory of God, His Son Jesus who has become Lord of my life and to The Holy Spirit for His continuing and constant reminders of how much God loves me and how much Jesus did for me. Thank you sir.

To my late mother Henrietta Alexander - you were right. Not many people will understand me but I am gonna be alright. Pastor Dingle (Aunt Vernice) has taken good care of me over the years just like you asked her too.

To my dad Willie Alexander (Edmond) - thanks Daddy for being a good dad and supporting me in all that is truly important to me. And definitely thank you for calling me pastor and understanding what it means to serve God through this vessel.

To my children, Anthony, Latoya and Bobby - it has not been easy at times. We went from God giving you to me and me giving you back to Him. Stay there and walk with him. Next to God you are my greatest loves, and like God I never would have made it without you. Parenting can be hard, thank you for making it a little easier.

And last but not least, my grandchildren. You are my pride and joy. Thank you for always wanting to spend time with me even if it's just so you can spend time with each other. I love you guys. And by the way, my name is Rolinda, but you can keep calling me Grandma Pastor Ro.

To my sister, Lessie, who has been my strongest advocate throughout life, thank you for loving me. To the rest of my family and church family, I never would have made it without God and you all.

Contents

Preface   9

Chapter 1:
An Encounter   13

Chapter 2:
My Story Is   17

Chapter 3:
As Time Goes By   21

Chapter 4:
Going Forward   27

Chapter 5:
Still Walking With Him   33

Chapter 6:
The Rest of the Story   37

Chapter 7:
Get Up and Listen   43

Chapter 8:
Wide Awake   49

Preface

As you travel with me through this book, I pray that the Holy Spirit will visit you as He has done with me so many times in the past and still does. May He lead and guide you in all truths and tell you everything that the Father has in store for you. In these visits I've learned that my destiny is not left up to chance but is left up to me. Knowing that God has preplanned my future has helped me to go through every tough issue in my life. **Jeremiah 29:11** states, *"For I know the thoughts I have towards you, saith the LORD, thoughts of peace and not evil, to give you an expected end."* So you see nothing just happens; your life has been predestined from the foundation of the Earth.

There is nothing that happens in your life that doesn't have a purpose or meaning. Never let anyone tell you that you are a mistake. You were purposed in the heart of God and conceived by your father in the womb of your mother to do great and mighty things through Christ Jesus. **Philippians 4:13** says, *"I can do all things through Christ which strengtheneth me."* Remember, the book of Genesis reminds us how we're created and why (see Genesis 1:27-28). So with that in mind go forth into your destiny.

Years ago God put a book in my heart entitled, "I Keep Giving Them My Heart." During the editing phase, my one and only copy was destroyed by a fire. Saddened and distraught, I put my pen down vowing to never write again. But it was not to be. Over the years I have attempted to rewrite that story over and over again. I even tried to write new books but for some reason I could never finish any of the manuscripts until now.

So on August 24, 2015, I was awakened earlier than usual and I knew then it was the time and season to write, "An Early Morning Visitor." The Holy Spirit started out by saying, "I'm glad you are here; let's get started as there is much work to do." Even though I will not be able to put all of my experiences in this book, I'm hoping that what I have chosen will help you through your journey in life. Remember, there is a book in all of us, whether we choose to write or tell it, the story must be told in order for others to overcome.

ALSO REMEMBER, PEOPLE THAT SEE US AS WE ARE CAN NEVER HANDLE WHERE WE'VE BEEN. SO BE CAREFUL THAT YOU DON'T ALLOW OTHERS' PERCEPTIONS TO BECOME YOUR OWN.

When we allow people to have power over us, we find that God has less power. In fact they become our God, because we allow them to control what we do or think. So what we are actually doing when we let others' thoughts control us is slowing down the process of our destiny which causes us to lose faith in God. When we don't have faith we don't have access to God and without Him everything is impossible for us. But once we take back our power from people and use their thoughts about us as stepping stones instead of stumbling blocks, we will soon realize that God being with us is better than the world against us.

Romans 8:31 says, *"What shall we then say to these things? If God be for us, who can be against us?"*

CHAPTER ONE
An Encounter

Before I move on to those early morning visits, let me tell you a little about my story and how I first met this visitor, who is really the Holy Spirit. Notice I said visitor and not stranger because I already knew Him. No one would ever let a stranger in their home to talk with them at that time of the morning, nor would they listen to what they had to say.

I recognized who He was, because I had met Him so many years earlier. He would try to talk to me but I wouldn't listen, and even if I did I wouldn't do what He was telling me to do. I didn't follow **James 1:22** which states *"But be ye doers of the word, and not hearers only, deceiving your own selves."*

Some people you meet in life you will never remember, others you will never forget, but my visitor was different. He wouldn't allow me to forget Him and He was always reminding me to remember who He was. He never talked about Himself but always talked to me about my Father. **John 14:26 says,** *"But the Comforter, which is the Holy Ghost, whom the Father will send in my name, he shall teach you all things, and bring all* *things to your remembrance, whatsoever I have said unto you."*

Like my big brother Jesus who is always doing the will of the Father, the Holy Spirit was always trying to remind me of what the Father's will is for my life. Our conversations were different than any other conversations that I had in prior relationships. I can remember going on a date where all the guy did was talk about himself, and even when he got around to talking about me, before I could respond he would find something else to say about himself. This encounter wasn't anything like that.

The Holy Spirit talked to me about things that happened earlier in my life that I did not understand, things that back then I did not think I could get through. He gently reminded me that even then God was with me and always would be no matter what I went through. So on this encounter I learned much about my Father that I didn't understand and about why I had gone through the things that I went through. In talking to Him I learned that everything I had gone through was for my good and to make me strong. **Romans 8:28 states,** *"and we know that all things work together for good to them that love God, to them who are the called according to his purpose."* In order for you to understand where I am going, it's going to be necessary to take you back to where I first met this visitor. You will find that as most of us did, I met Him as a child but I did not fully understand how important He

Early Morning Visitor

would become in my life and how many times I would need Him up until now. .

CHAPTER TWO
My Story Is

Have your children ever talked about an imaginary friend? Or maybe it was you that had the friend that no one could see. It could have been because you were lonely or didn't feel like you were part of the crowd. So you created this special person who was your friend and no one else's. Some would say it is okay to have a friend that no one else could see; others may think it's not a good idea. But as a young child I was introduced to a friend who I couldn't see and didn't know how to talk to, but let me assure you He was not imaginary. He was very real not only to me but to everyone who would take time to get to know Him.

I learned about Him in Sunday school at church. As I look back now, I think my Sunday school teacher saw something special in me. Talking with her today, I'm sure she did. While it seemed most other children had a lot of material possessions, my sister and I didn't. We lived with our grandparents. They didn't have a car so we didn't go many places. But on Sunday morning our neighbors would stop at the road, beep the horn, and we would go running out of the door excited about going to church. Now I didn't get a lot out of the morning service which started at 11:00 am because they seemed to quote a lot of scripture without explaining what the scripture meant, but it was something about Sunday school that made me want to get to know God more. I remember having to read stories each week and at the end of each lesson we would have to answer questions. I looked forward to sitting down on Saturday afternoon reading my lessons and then answering the questions. I remember there were four classes of books: primary, intermediate, junior and senior. I remember getting through the first two books but I'm not completely sure what happened with the other two.

I was always ready to participate in class, never shy, and always sure of my answers as if I had a special gift. When I gave the right responses, I had such a good feeling which now I know as joy. **Nehemiah 8:10b tells us** *"for the joy of the LORD is your strength."* I had developed a passion for the Word of God and when you love something you will do all you can to be good at it and that's just what I did!

As the years went by I grew in the Word of God and I grew up as well. I experienced hurts and disappointments that I didn't know how to get through because I only knew my friend in church and didn't know how to bring Him home with me. I struggled through many things.

Early Morning Visitor

Some summers my sister and I went to stay with our mom and dad who had busied their life with raising my cousin. Our clothes were packed and we anxiously waited for our parents to pick us up. We piled into the car but as we drove away from my grandma's house, I realized something was missing. Of course I would miss my grandma and granddaddy, but that wasn't it. Though I was happy to be with my parents, I still felt a sense of loneliness. It wasn't until recently that I realized why.

It was because I didn't take my friend with me and it would be an entire two months before I would talk to Him again. During the summers we didn't go to church at my parents' house like we did back home. And even though my grandparents didn't attend they always made sure we did.

We had a wonderful time as usual, but the day came when our vacation was over and it was time to return home. It was almost like leaving a dream and returning back to reality. The excitement we felt going was as real as the sadness we felt leaving.

CHAPTER THREE
As Time Goes By

A few more years passed by and I was about to become a 15 year old teenager even though I acted as if I was 21. My sister who was my best friend had become pregnant and was soon to be married. I felt more alone than ever before. Just when I thought nothing else could happen to shake my world something did. My grandmother who had always been in my life was now on her way to the hospital and I was so afraid because nobody seemed to know what was going on. Because it had been so long since I talked to my friend, I figured there was no use in praying. God wasn't hearing me and it seemed as if He wasn't talking to me either. So as we waited for what seem to be an eternity, things took a turn for the worst.

I remembered my aunt, who now lives with me, waking me up and saying, "Ro, I need you to go with me to the hospital to see Ma." I was so upset because it was the last day of school and I wanted to be able to tell my friends goodbye because I knew I wouldn't see them during the summer. But my aunt said no, so we took the bus to the hospital. I was angry and I cried to myself. But when I arrived at the hospital and saw my grandma lying on the bed unresponsive and looking frail, I was overcome with emotion. I felt so bad about the way I acted. Now the only grandmother I've known was dying and I wasn't sure if I could handle it. I didn't know how to pray or how to talk to God about what I was feeling. I couldn't call on my friend, the Holy Spirit, because the older I got the less time I had been spending at church.

So I just waited and finally the day came that she passed away. Through hurt and confusion, I kept hearing everyone say she had gone home to be with the Lord and that she wasn't suffering anymore. I felt a peace because I remembered talking about dying in Sunday school and how when we die we would go home to be with Jesus. I wondered if when my grandma met God, He would ask about me. Soon after that we buried her and so many decisions had to be made. I was finally going to live with my mother and father and even though I was happy, I still felt a bit of sadness over the loss of my grandma. Nothing would ever be the same ... not even me.

Once I arrived in New Jersey where my parents lived I would face a new set of challenges. After summer vacation I would be in the 11th grade. Everything was different – the people at school and even at church. My parents had started going to church so I thought I would have an encounter with the Holy Spirit again. The first week of school would prove to be more than I wanted to deal with because I didn't talk or dress like the other kids; I felt like an outcast. I needed my friend more now

Early Morning Visitor

than ever. The other kids teased me trying to make me ashamed of being from the country. I never knew there was anything wrong with being from the South. If anyone thinks the color of your skin makes a difference, just imagine compounding that with a very noticeable southern accent. After this there would be a lot of firsts in my life. The first time I would be without my grandparents, the first time I would live with my parents full time, the first time someone made me feel I was different, and the first time learning how cruel kids could be. I felt lost and alone again. It seemed as though my parents didn't understand what I was going through and that made it even harder. A point I would like to make here is that if you have children, always be there for their firsts and try to understand what they are going through.

Later in life I would learn that the devil always wants you to feel alone. He wants you to think nobody understands or cares about you. He tries to get you to believe that what you think and what you're going through is not important to God. DON'T BELIEVE THE HYPE! If I had brought my friend along He would have probably reminded me of what I remembered reading in **2 Corinthians 2:11** which says, *"Lest Satan should get an advantage of us: for we are not ignorant of his devices,"* and also that God promised to stay with us according to **Hebrews 13:5b** which reads, *"I will never leave you or forsake you."* What I didn't know was that my friend had come with me but I just wasn't hearing Him nor was I talking to Him because I thought He was no longer there.

The next two years of my life would be very different. I would face obstacles that every teenager faced but without my friend they seemed so much bigger than life itself. You see, I wasn't the pretty girl nor was I the light skinned girl with the good hair that all the boys seemed to be interested in. However, I wasn't the ugly duckling either.

I had a very shapely body even at a young age. As a side note young ladies, if you don't know how to take control of your bodies the enemy will convince you that your body is your own and you can do what you want to with it. STOP! This is not true, for the Bible states in **1 Corinthians 6:19,** *"What? Know ye not that your body is the temple of the Holy Ghost which is in you, which ye have of God, and ye are not your own?"* A lot of experiences I would have avoided had I been listening to my friend gently whispering in my ear even though the intensity sounded like He was screaming. He was speaking to me saying, "Don't do that! God loves you! He cares so much about you!" Yet I ignored His voice. There are going to be times that people are going to try and convince us to do things that we are uncomfortable with or that we know is wrong. Our friends may try to convince us that it is okay to smoke and drink. Young men are going to try to convince us that they love us and that it's okay for us to have sex with them because it will show them how much we love them. But it's not okay!

Even though I felt my friend was still in Virginia in that small church, He wasn't. He was right there with me. He was in my heart even though I did not fully understand it, and every now and again I would feel His presence.

During high school, I met two girls and we became the best of friends. It was interesting because the girls were related – they were aunt and niece even though they were around the same age. We finished that last year and a half together and graduated. It would be many years and many churches later but I found my friend again and this time I learned how to take Him home. I learned how to talk with Him and how to apply what we talked about to my life. Would there be days that the enemy tried to convince me that He wasn't there? Of course there were. But by this time I had matured and learned so much that his tactics were futile. I must say that you cannot simply just read the Word of God; you have to understand what you have read. This knowledge will come through faithfully attending a Bible-based teaching ministry. Going to church on Sundays is simply not enough, but attending Bible study where the Word of God is explained will help you to understand. **Proverbs 4:7** states that, *"Wisdom is the principal thing; therefore get wisdom: and with all thy getting get understanding."*

Before we end this chapter, I should let you know that you will have another visitor and he has no special time that he shows up. He will appear at any time and always tries to convince you that your real friend Jesus and your real comforter, the Holy Ghost doesn't care. This visitor that I'm speaking about is the devil. He is referred to by many names including Satan, snake, and serpent (see Revelation 12:9).

Don't ever believe his lies. Nothing he says is true. He only came for three things and none of them had to do with God. **John 10:10** says, *"The thief cometh not, but for to steal, and to kill, and to destroy: I am come that they might have life, and that they might have it more abundantly."* What does the devil want to kill, steal, and destroy? He wants to steal your faith, kill you, and destroy your belief in Jesus among other things. Remind him that though he came for those things, Jesus came that we have life and have it more abundantly!

CHAPTER FOUR
Going Forward

After I graduated from high school, I was considered an adult and it was time for me to be on my own. But the closer I got to that happening the more apprehensive I became. All sorts of questions began to bombard my mind. Can I really make it on my own? What if I fail? Should I change my plans and just stay at home? Home, which once felt like a prison to me, now sounded pretty good. What I thought was boxing me in and holding me back now seemed more like a safe haven or security blanket. Was I really ready to leave my parents' home? All of these thoughts were floating through my head, but there was no turning back now.

The road I had chosen wouldn't be an easy one. As a matter of fact it was not one that my parents wanted me to take but I had made up my mind. I hadn't prayed about it or really discussed it with anyone. And I sure hadn't talk to my friend about it, and at this time praying about something didn't seem to be an option. I had actually graduated with no specific goal in mind. I decided to take the summer off after graduation and figure out what I would do next. One day while riding the bus to a job which I knew was not my future, I felt an emptiness, a longing to talk with my friend. This time He didn't show up or at least that's what the devil wanted me to believe.

So I joined the United States Army. I decided this was best for me. However, I was almost angry at God because I thought He wasn't talking to me but it was me who actually wasn't listening. **John 10:27** says, *"For my sheep hear my voice, and I know them, and they follow me."* Up until now I had been listening to my own voice instead of the voice of God, which comes in the form of the Holy Spirit. I wasn't seeking God before making decisions even though the Bible declares in **Matthew 6:33,** *"But seek ye first the kingdom of God, and his righteousness; and all these things shall be added unto you."* **Proverbs 8:17** says, *"I love them that love me; and those that seek me early shall find me."* **Hebrews 11:6** states, *"But without faith it is impossible to please him: for he that cometh to God must believe that he is, and that he is a rewarder of them that diligently seek Him."* Now with all that Word about seeking God you would have thought that there was no way I could miss God. But you can and I did! Not only had I stopped seeking God, but without really even knowing it, I had also stopped trusting Him.

I can assure you that I would eventually come to my senses and realize who my Father was just like the prodigal son in **Luke 15:17–18.** *"And when he came to himself, he said, How many hired servants of my* *father's have bread enough and to spare, and I perish with hunger! I will arise and go to my father, and will say unto him, Father, I have sinned against heaven, and before thee."* Biblically speaking, until you realize who you are and who you belong to, you will be just like that son - lost and without your inheritance. You must understand that you belong to the Most High God and He is responsible for taking care of you. But please remember all you have to do is remind yourself of that, recognize it, and come back home.

I began to talk with Him again but it was more of me talking and Him listening. It was such a good feeling to be in His presence again, but like most things it would come to an end for a season. I would find myself in places and situations that I knew didn't please Him. And even though I didn't want to hurt or displease God, I often did. **Romans 7:15** says, *"For that which I do, I allow not: for what I would, that do I not; but what I hate, that do I."*

I fell into such a state of darkness. I was in a strange country; I didn't know anyone and my family was far away. I thought to myself I don't have to be lonely. That's when I decided that if I had a child I would have someone to love and someone who loved me. I did not intentionally plan to become pregnant, but I did hope it would happen. And it did. I wasn't married but I became pregnant. I was sure that this would make life easier and more fulfilling. I was so excited about what was about to happen I didn't seem to need my friend.

My oldest son was born that year and he was the most handsome boy I'd ever seen. He was mine and I was his, and the relationship that I was trying to build with him should have been the same type of relationship I was building with God.

Isn't it funny how we try to replace our relationship with God with other things and other people? So for this season, life would be about me and my son. Very shortly after his birth I would marry his father who loved someone else deep in his heart but most of all didn't love Jesus. My son and I would attend church on Sundays but his father never did, so after a while we didn't go either. I believed I had everything I ever needed: a husband, a child, a house, and a car, but I left out Jesus which was foolish of me because **Matthew 24:35** exclaims that, *"Heaven and Earth shall pass away, but my words shall not pass away."*

Later that year I became pregnant again and had fraternal twins – a boy and a girl – so now it seemed my life was really complete. I had all I wanted and little of what I actually needed. My life was like a fairy tale, but unlike fairy tales we didn't live happily ever after.

So I decided enough was enough. I had done it my way and now it was time to do it God's way. I rededicated my life to God and began to walk down the road with Him by my side. But the road wasn't always smooth! There were plenty of bumps and turns but God was right there with me.

So with the support of my family and a few close friends I decided I'd had enough and it was time to fully commit my life to God by doing what I had known from a child I was supposed to do. I mentioned earlier about that special understanding that I used to have in Sunday school. It wasn't just a feeling but it was the anointing of God calling and equipping me to preach the good news of the gospel. The spirit of God was on me. **Isaiah 61:1** states that, ***"The Spirit of the Lord GOD is upon me; because the LORD hath anointed me to preach good tidings unto the meek; he hath sent me to bind up the brokenhearted, to proclaim liberty to the captives, and the opening of the prison to them that are bound."*** I am so thankful that God was patient with me. Had it not been for His compassion and love this book would have been written by someone else. One thing I have learned during my walk with God is the vision will always be accomplished whether He uses us or someone else. **Habakkuk 2:3** declares, ***"For the vision is yet for an appointed time, but at the end it shall speak, and not lie: though it tarry, wait for it; because it will surely come, it will not tarry."***

Sometimes when we think God is saying no, He's actually saying wait awhile. God knows everything about us, and He only wants what's best for us. We have to learn how to trust God and wait on Him no matter what. Here's two scriptures that helped me, hopefully they will help you too.

Proverbs 3:5, *"Trust in the LORD with all thine heart; and lean not unto thine own understanding."*

Psalms 27:14, *"Wait on the LORD: be of good courage, and he shall strengthen thine heart: wait, I say, on the LORD."*

CHAPTER FIVE
Still Walking With Him

More years have gone by and my friend, the Holy Spirit, and I are still walking together. There have been many ups and downs but through it all He has been faithful. There have been times I wanted to give up but He was always there to remind me and encourage me not to. It's like I can hear him now saying, "Be patient my daughter, your Father is still in control."

I think waiting has been one of my biggest challenges in my walk with God. But I have always depended on the Word of God to get me through. One of my most favorite scripture that deals with waiting can be found in **Isaiah 40:31** which says, *"But they that wait upon the L*ORD* shall renew their strength; they shall mount up with wings as eagles; they shall run, and not be weary; and they shall walk, and not faint."*

Being in the military has definitely helped me in my walk because of the discipline I've learned. From the time I joined the military until the time I left the military twenty years later, I was always taught and trained to obey without question. Just like man's army, God's army requires us to be disciplined as well. In other words, God requires that we follow Him obediently in every area of our lives. Just as Noah built the Ark in obedience without question (see Genesis 6:12-21) and Abram moved his family (see Genesis 12: 1-4), we should willing follow the voice of God in our lives. It's been almost 20 years since I fully committed my life to God, and my children and I have learned how to lean on Jesus. Unlike my childhood, I did not send them to church to get to know God, but I went with them. So while they were being introduced to Him, I was building on what I already knew.

So let me encourage you to never give up on God because He is faithful and His promises are yea and amen. None of His words will go and return to Him incomplete. Please let the following scriptures bless you.

Hebrew 10:23, *"Let us hold fast the profession of our faith without wavering; (for he is faithful that promised)"*

2 Corinthians 1:20, *"For all the promises of God in him are yea, and in him Amen, unto the glory of God by us."*

Isaiah 55:11, *"So shall my word be that goeth forth out of my mouth: it shall not return unto me void, but it shall accomplish that which I please, and it shall prosper in the thing whereto I sent it."*

Please don't think that my life has been all bad, because walking with God has yielded great rewards and pleasures. I've had the opportunity to watch my kids grow up and see the birth of my grandchildren. I've come from thinking I couldn't do anything to realizing what the Bible declares in **Philippians 4:13** which states, *"I can do all things through Christ which strengtheneth me."* And if I can do it you can too.

One of my biggest accomplishments was retiring from the military because I know that without God it would not have happened. During the hard times when I had to be separated from my family and friends He strengthened me and made those times bearable. His Word reminds us of this when we read scriptures like **Matthew 19:26** that says, *"But Jesus beheld them, and said unto them, With men this is impossible; but with God all things are possible."* Looking at my life only lets you know that no matter how many times we fall or miss the mark, with His help we will always get back up and continue down the right road.

Another season of my life is about to come to an end. I have retired from the military and now I am embarking on what seems to me as unfamiliar territory. I am entering the civilian world and without the rigid structure of the military it would prove to be challenging. Being taught not to question and have others question me would challenge who I had become. I can tell you that though each season brings different things in our life they only represent the process we go through to get to what God ultimately has planned for our lives. There are times in my life that I experienced tragedies such as the passing of my grandmother, loneliness by being separated from my family, and even broken relationships, but they all helped me to realize that God was able to help me endure the heartache from each season.

A lot of times we become frustrated because of where we are in life. We are often confused by what we are going through and frustrated because we don't understand. Well can I help you with this? Knowing the season of God is important. As explained in **Ecclesiastes 3:1-8**, *"there is a season and a time for every purpose under the heaven ... "* The circumstance you may be in or going through right now is just a season according to God's timing to help strengthen and prepare you.

So you can see up until now God has always been by my side even when I didn't realize it. And guess what? He truly is the Alpha and Omega because He's still here (see Revelation 22:13).

CHAPTER SIX
The Rest of the Story

I'm now 57 years old and my relationship with God has been the longest relationship I've ever been. Not only is it the longest but it's been the best. Having been in many relationships and having gone through many situations I am just now looking back and realizing that God truly is the author and finisher of my faith (see Hebrews 12:2). No matter how many of those other relationships didn't work out, my relationship with God remained intact because of His love for me. I'm single now and have been married in the past. Even though the marriage did not work out, what it produced did. Out of the broken marriage came three wonderful children: Anthony, LaToya, and Bobby. And from them came eight wonderful grandchildren: Christian, Anthony Jr, Jordyn, Brian Jr, Bobby III, Janiyah, Joshua, and Jada.

So you see pain does birth joy. Even though I didn't write that wonderful song "From Pain to Joy," I can relate to it. Now I'm not sure who Betty Wright was singing about when she wrote this song, but when I used to listen to it, it made me think about Jesus. He was the one who took me from pain to joy. When I could have given up and threw in the towel He reminded me of what

His Son went through on the Cross and nothing that I had gone through compared to that. I came from being an unhappy teenager, a lonely young adult, to being who I am in God right now – a virtuous woman. Proverbs 31 talks about finding a virtuous woman. I believe we can all find her because she lives in us (read Proverbs 31 in its entirety). Even though the Holy Spirit and I talked about my broken relationships, He never seemed to dwell there and never wanted me to either. I believe when the Word says in **John 8:36**, *"If the Son therefore shall make you free, ye shall be free indeed,"* that He was definitely talking about me.

Now that I'm back in relationship and fellowship with the Lord wholeheartedly, I try to make sure we keep in contact on a regular basis. Over the years I realize that I couldn't have made it without Him. So many times I have wanted to give up but He never would let me. He was always there to say these words to me: "***You can do all things through Christ which strengthens you***" (see Philippians 4:13). He would also say, "*.**No weapon that is formed against thee shall prosper; and every tongue that shall rise against thee in judgment thou shalt condemn. This is the heritage of the servants of the* Lord, *and their righteousness is of me, saith the Lord*" (Isaiah 54:17). Now how could I not win with a coach like that!

No matter where you come from or who you are it does not determine where you will go and who you will become. I know people will try to convince you of what you can't do instead of encouraging you that you can, but remember you belong to the LORD and HE is in control. **Jeremiah 32:27** reminds us of this: *"Behold, I am the LORD, the God of all flesh: is there any thing too hard for me."* Not only is He the God of all mankind, He's your God and He wants what's best for you. Jeremiah 29:11 says *"For I know the thoughts that I think toward you, saith the Lord, thoughts of peace, and not of evil, to give you an expected end."* The Word of God also tells us not to despise or look down on small beginnings because it won't always be that way.

The Word also lets us know that our latter days shall be greater: *"Though thy beginning was small, yet thy latter end should greatly increase"* (Job 8:7). And the reason why that's important to me is because I'm in the latter days and they have proven to be so much better. For now I am stronger and I am wiser and nothing seems impossible to me. I live, learn, and grow as I continue to get up early in the morning and talk with my friend who will now no longer be nameless. His name is Jesus and He speaks to me through the Holy Spirit. As a little girl in Boydton, VA, the Holy Spirit started speaking to me, and I'm so glad. No matter how many times I walked away from Him, He never walked away from me and was always found in the same place – in my heart. Now that little girl has become a mother, grandmother, and even a pastor, and is still talking to that early morning visitor, my friend the Holy Spirit.

I want to share with you some of what He has been saying to me lately. Please know that the hardest times in our lives were the closest times with God because in our weakest moments He became our strength. His strength helps us in our weakness. Though times get hard and obstacles seem unmovable, He continuously encourages us through His Word. In **2 Corinthians 12:9** it reads, *"And he said unto me, My grace is sufficient for thee: for my strength is made perfect in weakness…"* As many times as He found my heart broken and my feelings and emotions crushed, whenever I decided to get up from the fall, He was always there to pick me up. There were times I found myself making mistakes and not living up to the expectation of God, but I got up and I moved on just as the Word declares in **Proverbs 24:16** states, *"For a just man falleth seven times, and riseth up again."* So just man, just woman, keep getting up. Continue in the race.

At times I've felt broken beyond repair and too far away from the shore to be saved, but I can always remember Him encouraging me that I could make it. Often times it was expressed in a song or the lyrics to a poem that He gives me that is birthed out of pain but written out of victory.

Early Morning Visitor

"Oh Lord I Can't Go On"

Oh GOD I can't go on LORD
The mountains are too steep
But then I hear you whisper
I'm the Shepherd and you're my sheep

Oh GOD I can't go on LORD
The burdens too heavy to bear
And still I hear you whispering
You can because I care

Oh GOD I can't go on LORD
The road just twists and turns
And still I hear you whisper
It's patience you will learn

Oh GOD I can't go on LORD
The battle's too hard to fight
And still I hear you whisper
By My Spirit not your might

Oh GOD I can't go on LORD
The troubles just won't cease
And still I hear you whisper
It's in Me you'll find your peace

Oh GOD I can't go on LORD
I can't seem to past the test
But this time I can hear you say
Come home you've earned your rest.

~Rolinda Butler

CHAPTER SEVEN:
Get Up and Listen

The Holy Spirit shows up sometimes at 3:00 AM, sometimes earlier depending on how much time I've spent with Him the day before. He is never late and is always a gentleman. He is never loud or overpowering but always courteous. Even though there have been times when He has shown up and I have not let Him in, He never seemed to be offended but would come back the next day. I am so thankful He is not like man, because if He was I would never have been able to complete this work.

I would have all kinds of excuses why He couldn't come in and visit, so many I won't even mention them. I would find myself going back to the Cross experience. He reminded me that when it was Jesus' time to die for me, He didn't come up with an excuse why He couldn't; He just did it. So my excuses didn't matter because Jesus took all of our excuses to the Cross. Even still, during the times when I "stood Him up," I assure you He has never given up on me, and faithfully shows up no matter what.

At times I would wonder why. And with much patience the Holy Spirit would answer and say, "My daughter you deserve this and more; the Father through the Son made sure of this. Remember, when He died on the cross it was not just for what you did, it was for what you are doing and will do in the future. Grace and mercy walk hand in hand and show up just when you need them most. As a matter of fact they came along that day you didn't commune with Me, but because the Father already knew what you were going to do, He decided to give you another chance." **Lamentations 3:22-23** states, *"It is the LORD's mercies that we are not consumed, because his compassions fail not. They are new every morning: great is thy faithfulness."* **Psalm 23:6** says, *"Surely goodness and mercy shall follow me all the days of my life: and I will dwell in the house of the LORD for ever."* No matter how many times we mess up God's goodness and His mercy will never ever run out.

Oftentimes on our Christian journey we don't make time to talk with God. We do what I'd like to refer to as a "drive-by." You know that's when you're on the way out the door to your job but you don't have time to stop and talk with God so you say a quick "thank you Lord." And then when lunch time rolls around we are still busy with the job at hand. But as the day goes on and things don't seem to be going as we expect, we look up and ask God this question: Why didn't you tell me or why didn't you help me? Why didn't you stop me? And then we hear that still small voice say, "My daughter you didn't ask Me." My son you didn't seek Me. The scripture clearly tells us in **Luke 11:9** says, *"And I say unto you,*

Ask, and it shall be given you; seek, and ye shall find; knock, and it shall be opened unto you." God wants us to seek Him daily and He also wants us to dwell in His presence. **John 15:7** declares that, *"If ye abide in me, and my words abide in you, ye shall ask what ye will, and it shall be done unto you."* Now to abide in Him and allow Him to abide in us means we must spend time in the Word of God and then allow His Word to live in us. We can't just glance over the Word, but we must study the Word daily. Joshua 1:8 reminds us that we must meditate on His Word and do what is written in His Word which would cause us to prosper and have good success. If we seek Him early and often, we will find Him for the Bible declares that He is a rewarder of them that diligently seek Him (see Hebrews 11:6).

So I learned a lot about studying the Word of God and meditating on it so that I could be closer to Him. I also learned that it pleased God. God loves it when we study His Word, because in doing so we are showing Him how much we love Him. In **2 Timothy 2:15** it clearly states if we want God's approval we must study: *"Study to shew thyself approved unto God, a workman that needeth not to be ashamed, rightly dividing the word of truth."*

Now most of us think of an early morning visitor as an inconvenience and would probably be very upset if someone showed up at our house at such an ungodly hour. We would consider it rude and inconsiderate for someone to come over to our home without an invitation. But what we neglected to remember is that the Holy Spirit has an open invitation. When we accepted Him as Lord and Savior of our life we gave Him access to our heart and our home. **Romans 10:9-10** states this: *"That if thou shall confess with thy mouth the Lord Jesus, and shalt believe in thine heart that God hath raised him from the dead, thou shalt be saved. For with the heart man believeth unto righteousness; and with the mouth confession is made unto salvation."* Do you remember the day that someone prayed for you to get saved and you repeated that scripture, and at the end of that prayer you invited Jesus to come into your life? That was the day you made Him Lord and Savior of your life. Aren't you glad? And if you haven't you can take time out right now and make Him your own. Just talk to Him and let Him know that you desire to change and want to reign with Him in His kingdom now and forever more.

So don't be concerned how you look or what are wearing. If He comes just open the door of your heart and let Him in. Have you ever heard anyone say this: "Please don't talk to me until I've had my morning cup of coffee," and you see them around 11:00 AM and they still need a cup? Well maybe they should turn that morning cup of coffee into a morning cup of Jesus. Unlike instant coffee, Jesus is more like coffee that must be brewed. You see it is a process we must go through in order to know Him. Now knowing Him involves learning about Him and how good

Early Morning Visitor

He really is. Remember Maxwell House Coffee whose slogan is "Good to the Last Drop." I can assure you He is so much better than Maxwell House. Maxwell House may run out, but God never will.

CHAPTER EIGHT
Wide Awake

It's about 3:00 AM and I am wide awake and anxiously awaiting for my time with Him. I find now that instead of being aggravated about the possible loss of sleep, I'm actually in a state of expectation because I know when He arrives, He will not only give me my plan for the day, but He will tell me about many things that He has heard the Father say concerning me. We will talk about things that happened the day before and concerning the day ahead, He would always say, "Your Father has it all in control so don't worry, just put your trust in God." Now the scripture tells us in **Proverbs 3:5**, *"Trust in the Lord with all your heart, lean not to you own understanding."* This means that no matter what happens in our lives we must have confidence in God and in His ability to keep us and protect us. That's my sister's favorite scripture. No matter what comes up or what you go through, you have to trust Him. She trusted Him and He brought her through cancer. She overcame cancer because she trusted Him! (see Hebrews 10:35)

Now that I'm awake, I will get my instructions as a pastor and also will get a word for the people of God in the ministry. The Holy Spirit uses this time to inform me and remind me of things that the Father wants me to do in order for me to accomplish the task He has given me. Not only does He share with me, but He allows me to share with Him and He listens to every word. Out of His mouth always comes the wisdom of God. He never says anything on His own but only says what He has heard the Father say. Through talking with Him I have learned how to get the will of God to manifest in my life. He gives me knowledge but not just any knowledge; it is revelation knowledge which is ultimately the wisdom of God. I've learned how to pray the will of God unselfishly always wanting His will and not mine to be done. Matthew 6:10 reminds us that the will of God is to be done on Earth as it is in Heaven. In other words when we pray, we need to pray according to the Word of God which is the Will of God, even if it's not what we desire. The Word also tells us in Luke 22:42 that even Jesus when He was on the mountain prayed for God to deliver Him but He understood that it was more important that God's will be done and not His own.

There have been times that I haven't gotten everything right nor have I finished all of my assignments but the Holy Spirit reminds me that the Word states in Matthew 25:21, if I'm faithful over a few things He will make me ruler over many. Not only will He do that but he is also willing to forgive me and forget the things that I have done that were not pleasing to Him. In 1 John 1:9 we are reminded that if we ask for forgiveness He is faithful and just to forgive us of our sins and throw them away never remembering them again.

I've also learned just how much the Father loves me. Even though I know He does, it still feels good when I hear Him say it in His Word. You see when you're in a relationship no matter how much someone does things for you to show they love you, it stills feels good to hear them say they love you. During the course of my life I have loved many and been loved by few, but none compared to the love that God has for me. The Word of God tells us that no man loves us more than God because he proved it by laying down His life for us because He considered us His friends (see John 15:13). When people in the world love us, often it is conditional and based on how they feel and what we do. In many cases, the love of the world has to be earned, but the love that comes from God is pure and eternal. It is longsuffering, non-judgmental, and is given freely without cost to us.

I asked Him why He comes so early and He replied with such boldness and confidence yet with that same still small voice saying, "Because the Father misses you and wants to talk with you." I replied, "Why hasn't He?" He responded, "It's like this – remember those days when you would rush from the house and promise to spend time with God when you got home but something always came up. He was trying to talk to you then." Sadly I lowered my head because everything He said was true. I had been so busy with all that I thought was important, I had neglected the most important thing of all and that was my time with God.

I had begun to treat God like I would treat a client, making appointments that sometimes my schedule would not allow me to keep. And I would hear myself saying, "Can I reschedule" or "I will get back to you," which had become my favorite line. You see the world and all things in it have become too important in our lives. I'm not a real fan of Social Media Networks, but it seems like it's the only way the Holy Spirit can get a word to some people. He has to send a friend request, but will we accept Him? Or if He inboxes us will we respond?

Imagine one day God trying to get in touch with you and He hears something like this: "God bless you, you have reached the voicemail of (your name). I'm not available right now, but if you leave your name, number, and a brief message I will get back to you at my earliest convenience." Or can you imagine using the key on your phone to block a call from Him. Well that's what we are saying and doing when we do not take time to talk with Him and more importantly, listen to Him.

Here are a couple of verses to help you with this: ***"Be still, and know that I am God …"*** (Psalm 46:10) and ***"to day if ye will hear his voice, harden not your hearts …"*** (Hebrews 3:15). These scriptures remind us how important it is to take the time to get to know God and to listen to what He has to say, because in those times we will find instructions for success in our lives.

So now I have learned to get up when I wake up early and prepare myself for a visit that I know that will bring me such joy and peace. And if it means getting up earlier I'm actually okay with that. It's quiet and not a lot of people are up at that time of the morning. So our visits and our talks are usually uninterrupted. Now the enemy doesn't sleep but at this time of the morning he seems to be less active in my life. It is probably because he is plotting his next move against me. However, I'm not worried because I understand that the Holy Spirit will let me know. In **2 Corinthians 2:11** it states, ***"Lest Satan should get an advantage of us: for we are not ignorant of his devices."*** God will always let us know through the Holy Spirit what the enemy has planned in our lives. With this knowledge we are able to defeat him because we know his plan.

I've learned so much from my friend – things I thought I would never have understood. In His presence is the fullness of joy. I'm not talking about a happy place; I'm talking about a true place of power and strength. Remember, the joy of the Lord is our strength. You see it is at these times that I spend with the Spirit of God that nothing bothers me and when I come out of these sessions with Him, I am strengthened and encouraged.

I still continue to wake up early but now instead of trying to turn over and sleep I get up, listen, and commune with Him knowing that what He is about to say to me is just what I need to start my day. I used to think the reason I was waking up early was because I was worried about something or I had went to bed too early. But that wasn't the reason at all. The Holy Spirit was waking me up to spend some quality time with me. So that I won't be up by myself and now that you know who my visitor is and why He comes, would it be okay if I sent Him to your house by the way of this prayer?

Father God, in the Precious Name of Jesus, I come to you Lord. Forgive me of my sins, throw them into the sea to remember them no more. With my mouth I confess that Jesus is the only begotten Son of the Father. He died and rose with all power in His hands, and that He died for me so that I would have access to the Father. I realize that You gave us your Son and your Son gave us His Life and He is the only way to get to You. I accept Him as Lord and Savior of my life and by faith I believe I am saved.

In Jesus' Name

Amen

If you prayed that prayer and believed it with your whole heart you are saved. Now look forward to many visits of your own. It may not be as early as mine but they will be as wonderful.

There may be some of you that are saved, but still struggling with the storms of life. At times it may seem as if you are alone and by yourself. God wants you to know that He is a very present help in the time of trouble. The following prayer may help you to access the power of God through the Holy Spirit:

Lord I realize that it was necessary for You to go away in order for me to receive the promise of the Comforter and by faith I invite the Holy Spirit to dwell on the inside of me, teaching me all things and bringing all things to my remembrance.

In Jesus' Name

Amen

If you would be willing to get up early in the morning also, He will be more than willing to come by your house and talk to you too just as He wakes me up early to share things with me from our Father. Not only does He share with me but he allows me to share with Him my hopes, my dreams, and even my desires. Through talking with Him I've learned that my desires should line up with what has already been established in the Word.

Now let's talk about these desires a little bit. Our will must conform to the will of our Father and we must learn to pray what His words says. There will be times when it seems like the Father and you are on different wavelengths but remember what the scripture says about

His ways and our ways and His thoughts and our thoughts (see Isaiah. 55:8). Always remember God knows what's best for you and no good thing will He withhold from you (see Psalms 84:11). The scriptures also tell us in Romans 8:28 how all things work together for our good.

Spending time with God is not just an appointment or something you can change or cancel; it's an assignment. Like school, if you miss an assignment, you will fail or at the very least have to make it up or take the test again. Now I don't know about you but I don't want to repeat or have to do any assignments for a second time. I want to complete the task on time so that I won't have to stay after or be held back.

You may have purchased this book because of a need in your life and may not have time to read it but just as sure as I'm writing late at night and early in the morning you may find that that's when it's your time too. Reading this book is just an introduction to the Holy Spirit. He will soon become as real to you as He is to me. So before I end this book I want to share a few secrets about Him with you. He is sometimes referred to as the Comforter. **John 16:7** states, ***"Nevertheless I tell you the truth; It is expedient for you that I go away: for if I go not away, the Comforter will not come unto you; but if I depart, I will send him unto you."*** Jesus had to go away because if He didn't the Comforter (Holy Spirit) could not come. The first thing you need to know is He is a person and comforter who will live inside you. The second thing you need to know about Him is He gives you power. **Acts 1:8** says, *"But ye shall receive power, after that the Holy Ghost is come upon you: and ye shall be witnesses unto me both in Jerusalem, and in all Judaea, and in Samaria, and unto the uttermost part of the earth."*

The early morning visitor never talks about Himself but always talks about the one who sent Him to remind us about what was done for us as stated in **John 14:26**, *"But the Comforter, which is the Holy Ghost, whom the Father will send in my name, he shall teach you all things, and bring all things to your remembrance, whatsoever I have said unto you."*

Hopefully your visits with Him will begin now and will be as helpful to you as they have been to me. I can't imagine life without Him and as you get to know Him you won't be able to either. So please allow Him access to your life. Let Him lead you, guide you, and show you the way to your destiny. I can't tell you how many visits we had before I wrote this book, but I can tell you that there will be many more. Not many more books, but many more visits.

Hmmmm, is that a knock I hear? Maybe not. You may need to check the door of your spirit.

God Bless You

NOTES FOR YOUR EARLY MORNING VISITS

NOTES FOR YOUR EARLY MORNING VISITS

About the Author

Rolinda Butler is an international evangelist and teacher anointed by God who has travelled the world using her enlistment in the United States Army as a vehicle to spread the gospel wherever her assignments took her for over 20 years. Her unrelenting efforts to spread the gospel of peace led her into many different countries. Her teaching ministry style – simple yet effective – draws people of all ethnicities. Upon retiring from the military the call to pastor became more evident as her passion was to see broken people healed, delivered, and set free.

Rolinda's worst failures always turned into her greatest triumphs. Whether broken relationships or unions, she's always had an innate will to succeed. In the words of her late mother, Henrietta Alexander, spoken to her dear Aunt Vernice Dingle, "Watch out for her… she's different and people are not going to understand her." But being different has proven to be successful as that is what keeps her focused.

Pastor Butler is determined to help others fulfill their destiny by changing their thought process through the Word of God. There have been many mistakes made, but she found that in God His mercies are new every morning.

Pastor Butler has served as the founder and senior pastor of Awesome Faith Ministries in South Hill, VA since 1997. She has three adult children and eight grandchildren.

To contact the author for speaking engagements, conferences, book tours and signings, write

Visit www.earlymorningvisitor.com
E-mail: earlymorningvisit@gmail.com

Other Authors by
COOKE PUBLISHING HOUSE

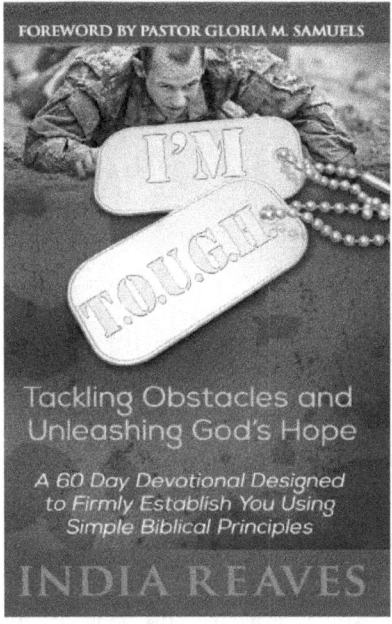

I'm T.O.U.G.H is a 60 day devotional book intended to resolutely ground the reader in a strong spiritual foundation. The messages in this book thrust the reader to think and reflect on their own lives and situations and to dig deep in themselves and be contingent on the victor that is in each and every one of us. Through scriptures, stories, personal testimonies, and teachings, readers will grasp hold to the fact that they are built to last.

ISBN: 978-0-6922-0263-0

For more information, visit
www.imtoughdevotional.com

Other Authors by
COOKE PUBLISHING HOUSE

Devastated But Not Destroyed is a divine interruption for those who may be headed towards destruction. It will jolt your faith, sustain your strength, and change your perspective from one of pity and pain to that of power. Discover how to master the moments of your life, pack up the pity party for good, and embrace the challenge of change. Everyone at some point will experience devastation, and this book serves as the go-to guide to rediscover the tenacity and fortitude necessary to avoid the pitfalls of destruction.

ISBN: 978-0-692-34201-5

For more information, visit
www.devastatedbutnotdestroyed.com

Other Authors by
COOKE PUBLISHING HOUSE

We speak of spiritual warfare in the same mindset as physical warfare. We have approached it with thoughts of violent and vehement confrontations. In actuality, spiritual warfare is best fought using simple biblical principles. 100 out of 100 people are offended, the offender, or both. This book is intended to teach one of the most basic, yet most powerful principles - and that is the principle of forgiveness. As you begin to practice this principle, you will experience a freedom in your spirit that you have longed to have.
ISBN: 978-0-692-30523-2

For more information, e-mail
scvinson@gmail.com

www.ingramcontent.com/pod-product-compliance
Lightning Source LLC
Chambersburg PA
CBHW070551300426
44113CB00011B/1869